faith in art

HANUKKAH

Valerie Evans

Acknowledgements

There are many acknowledgments to be made in the making of this book. Firstly, I would like to thank Peter Kellie, Sue Butcher and all the staff at Little Ealing Primary School, particularly Julie Claridge, Sabina Khan and Lucilla Gallagher for their help with the displays.

I would also like to thank Sabina Khan, Punam Mair and Annie Miller for reading through and checking the different chapters. I also owe thanks to Maurice, Suzannah and Grace Evans and Stephanie Cockburn for their creative contribution to this book. Finally, a special thank you to the very gifted children at Little Ealing Primary School whose colourful work fills this book.

Clay Buddhas (page 37)

© 2005 Folens on behalf of the author.

Belair Publications, Apex Business Centre, Boscombe Road, Dunstable, LU5 4RL.
Email: belair@belair-publications.co.uk

Commissioning editor: Zoë Nichols   Editor: Joanne Mitchell   Page Layout: Suzanne Ward and Patricia Hollingsworth
Photography: Kelvin Freeman   Cover Design: Steve West

Illustrations: Mark Airs pp9, 11; Alan Baker pp13, 19, 29, 43 (top left, middle left, bottom right), 49, 53 (top left, bottom); Jamil Dar pp23, 43 (top right, middle right); Vanessa Lubach p71; Emma McCann p41; Jim Peacock p53 (top right); Nicola Pearce pp55, 59; Peter Wilks pp27, 32, 65; Kirsty Wilson p23 (top right).

Poems:
p11 'God sends a rainbow after the rain' by Michael Forster from *The Children's Book of Poems, Prayers and Meditations* published by Element Books © Kevin Mayhew Ltd, Buxhall, Stowmarket, Suffolk, IP14 3BW, UK.
p27 'Mela' by Jean Kenward from *Let's Celebrate: Festival Poems* published by Oxford University Press.
p59 'Light the Festive Candles' from *Skip Around the Year* by Aileen Fisher. Copyright © 1967 Aileen Fisher. Used by permission of Marian Reiner.
p71 'Idh Mubarak!' by Berlie Doherty from *Let's Celebrate: Festival Poems* published by Oxford University Press.

Photos:
p42 *Prayer Wheel*, 1976 © Ric Ergenbright/CORBIS
p43 *Buddhism in Britain*, 2004 © Colin McPherson/CORBIS
p53 *Tallitim and Tefillin*, 2004 © Royalty-Free/CORBIS

First published in 2005 by Belair Publications.

British Library Cataloguing in Publication Data. A catalogue record for this publication is available from the British Library.

ISBN 0 94788 282 0

Contents

Introduction

It was Guru Nanak, a Sikh, who explained that God would neither judge people by the colour of their skin nor by their religion, but by their actions or deeds. He said that the world is like a mirror and it is up to individuals how they reflect in it. It is important for young children to learn about a variety of religions with their different beliefs, traditions and customs and to teach tolerance in the hope that the world will become a safer and more peaceful place.

Faith in Art offers a creative way to teach Religious Education in the classroom through art and display. Each chapter in the book covers a world religion – Christianity, Hinduism, Sikhism, Buddhism, Judaism and Islam. Themes within each chapter cover the different aspects of each faith – Beliefs, Places of Worship, Stories, Prayers and Paintings and Festivals and Ceremonies. Stories, prayers and paintings are reproduced and are intended to be used with the whole class or a small group as starting points when beginning a piece of artwork or a display.

I hope that this book offers plenty of creative ideas and gives children a clearer understanding of the different faiths and the realisation that their actions and deeds will make a difference.

Valerie Evans

Beliefs

Christians believe that everything was created by God. The name 'Christian' comes from their faith in Jesus Christ, the Son of God, who came down to earth to spread the word of God. Jesus was born in Bethlehem to a Jewish couple named Mary and Joseph. Mary had been told by the Angel Gabriel that she would give birth to a boy who would be the Son of God, and she accepted her conception by the power of God.

Dough Plaques

All Christians honour Mary as Jesus' mother, and Catholics and Orthodox Christians believe that if they pray to her she will plead to Jesus on their behalf. The image of Mary and baby Jesus is used on many religious artefacts.

Design some plaques showing Mary holding the baby Jesus.

Resources
- Plain flour, salt and water
- Mixing bowl, spoon and cup
- Non-stick baking tray
- Paints and paintbrushes
- Clay tools

Approach

1. Make up some salt dough using two cups of flour to every cup of salt used. Slowly add water to make a pliable dough – not too dry and not too sticky.

2. Flatten the dough with the palm of your hand and then, using a clay tool, cut into an arched shape.

3. Roll a small ball of dough into a strip and use as a border to the plaque. This can be joined by using water. Press designs into the dough border using the clay tools.

4. Put onto a non-stick baking tray and bake in a low oven (150°C) for 2–3 hours. Leave in the oven to cool.

5. Paint the design with Mary holding the baby Jesus onto the dough plaque.

Places of Worship

Christianity has grown to be the largest of all religions, and people of the Christian faith attend church services where they sing hymns and pray together. People attending a service are called the congregation. Most churches have a large main space called the nave for the congregation. The alter is housed in the chancel or sanctuary. The vestry is where the priest or vicar prepares for a service. Behind the altar is a screen painting or carved relief known as the altarpiece, often decorated with scenes from the Bible or images of saints. The vicar stands in the pulpit to deliver a sermon to the congregation, who also pray and sing hymns to the glory of God.

Model Church

On the roof of some churches there is a cockerel weather vane. This reminds Christians of the time when Peter, one of Jesus' disciples, denied being one of Jesus' followers three times. A cock crowed as Peter made his third denial, something that Jesus had foretold. Make a model of a church, putting in stained glass windows and adding a cockerel weather vane to the roof.

Resources
- Cardboard box and pieces of card
- Paints and paintbrushes
- A selection of different-coloured tissue paper
- Bin bags
- Masking tape
- Thin wooden sticks
- 3-D outliner
- PVA glue
- Modroc
- Water tray

Approach

1. Cut windows in the sides of the cardboard box.

2. Make either a tower or a church spire from the card and add to the building.

3. Make a roof from the card and cover the whole structure with strips of the modroc soaked in water for 2–3 seconds. Allow to dry and harden.

4. Using PVA glue, stick small, flat pieces of different-coloured tissue paper onto a section of the bin bag and peel off when dry.

5. Cut the tissue paper pieces into window shapes and stick into place using the masking tape.

6. Use a 3-D outliner to draw other windows and colour in with paint.

7. Paint the model of the church.

8. Cut out a cockerel from the card, stick onto a thin wooden stick and add to the church as shown.

Stained-glass Windows

Many churches are laid out in the shape of a cross to symbolise the cross on which Christ died and some have stained-glass windows depicting stories from the Bible. In the past, when people were unable to read and write, Bible stories would be told through the beautiful stained-glass windows in churches. The windows, still popular in modern churches, flood the interiors of many churches with spectacular coloured light.

Design a stained-glass window for a church or cathedral and display on the classroom window so that the natural light enhances the design.

Resources
- Paper and felt-tipped pens for display sketches
- Black bin bags
- A selection of different-coloured tissue paper
- PVA glue
- Chalk

Approach

1. Draw a design for the stained-glass window and colour in with felt-tipped pens.

2. Spread out a large, black bin bag and draw the design on the bin bag in chalk.

3. Cut or tear the tissue paper as required for the design. Put PVA glue on the bin bag and stick on the pieces of tissue paper to build up the design. Make sure that there are no gaps showing the black bin bag and leave the work to dry, ensuring that it remains flat.

4. Carefully peel the hardened tissue paper design from the plastic backing. Cut the design to fit individual window panes and fix in place. Alternatively, display in a glass door without cutting.

Stories and Prayers

Read the story on the opposite page to the class. Create a large class display showing Daniel in the lions' den. Make the lions' heads as masks so that they are removable and can be taken down and used for dramatising the story.

Daniel in the lions' den

Approach

1. Draw a lion's head onto the back of the sandpaper and cut out.

2. Using chalk, draw around the lion's head on the black bin bag.

3. Tear strips of different-coloured tissue paper and glue around the outline of the lion's face.

4. When dry, peel the ring of tissue paper from the bin bag backing and glue the sandpaper face into the middle.

Resources
- Black bin bags
- Sandpaper
- Brown, yellow and orange tissue paper
- PVA glue
- Large sheets of white sugar paper
- Paints and small sponges
- Black felt-tipped pens
- Chalk
- Elastic
- Oil pastels

5. Add the lion's features with a black felt-tipped pen or oil pastels.

6. Add elastic to the back of the mask.

7. Draw and paint the lion's body using small sponges on the sugar paper and cut out when dry.

8. Draw and paint the figure of Daniel to add to the collage.

9. Assemble the collage, adding the removable masks to the lions to complete the display.

Daniel in the lions' den

Daniel was a trusted friend and adviser to King Darius of Babylon. Darius always asked Daniel's advice about important matters, and when Daniel became governor of the whole kingdom the other governors were very angry and very jealous. They decided that the only way to get Daniel into trouble would be through his love of God and they decided on a plan to have him killed.

The governors went to King Darius and told him that he shouldn't tolerate anyone praying to a god rather than asking the king for help and guidance, and a law was passed. Although Daniel heard about this new law, he still prayed to his god. When the jealous governors heard Daniel's prayers, they told King Darius that Daniel must be thrown into the lions' den as the new law decreed.

Darius didn't want to harm Daniel, but he had to keep his word and follow the new law. As Daniel was taken to the lions' den, Darius whispered, 'I hope your god will keep you safe.' The lions didn't harm Daniel in any way and when he was released, Darius ordered that everyone should worship Daniel's god.

Noah's Ark

In the story of Noah's Ark, God floods the Earth to destroy everything bad in the world. His friend, Noah, was instructed to build an ark and save two of every kind of animal and bird. When the floodwaters eventually went down there could be a new start on Earth, and God stretched a huge rainbow across the sky to show that he would never again destroy the world that he had created. The rainbow remains a symbol that all creation matters to God.

Ark Display

Tell the story of Noah's Ark, read the poem by Michael Forster (see page 11), and discuss issues such as hope, fear, love and friendship. Make a model of Noah's Ark and a rainbow display with the children's poems and prayers written on painted rainbow paper.

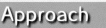

Approach

1. Paint over the A4 pieces of paper with water and then add arcs for the seven colours of the rainbow using drawing inks.

2. When dry, ask the children to write their own prayers on the sheets.

3. Paint a rainbow on a large sheet of sugar paper and cut out. Display the rainbow and the prayers on a display board. Add a dove and the figures of Noah and his wife.

4. Model an ark from clay, building up the shape using coils. Join the coils from the inside, but leave them visible from the outside to represent planks of wood.

5. Roll out the clay to approximately a two centimetre thickness. Using animal-shaped pastry cutters, cut two of each different animal. Using clay tools, add texture to show wool, fur and so on, on the different animals. Allow to dry and harden.

6. Add some animals to the ark, joining in place with clay tools. Allow to dry and harden.

7. Paint the ark and all of the animals and varnish as required.

Resources

- A4 white paper
- Rainbow-coloured drawing inks
- Paints and paintbrushes
- Air-drying clay
- Animal-shaped pastry cutters
- PVA glue
- Varnish
- Sugar paper
- Clay tools
- Rolling pins

God sends a rainbow after the rain,
colours of hope gleaming through pain;
bright arcs of red and indigo light,
making creation hopeful and bright.
Colours of hope dance in the sun,
while yet it rains the hope has begun;
colours of hope shine through the rain,
colours of love, nothing is vain.
When we are lonely, when we're afraid,
though it seems dark, rainbows are made;
even when life itself has to end,
God is our rainbow, God is our friend.

Michael Forster

Festivals and Ceremonies

Christmas celebrates Jesus' birth, when his parents, Mary and Joseph, travelled to Bethlehem to comply with a census ordered at that time. The Christmas story of Jesus born in a stable because all the inns were full, is retold in songs, pictures and dramas throughout the world. The story of the birth of Jesus is called the Nativity.

Nativity Collage

Make three fabric collages with backgrounds of different-textured wools to depict the Christmas story. One collage can show an angel telling the shepherds news of Jesus' birth, one can show Jesus' birth in the stable and the third can show the wise men from the east with their gifts for the baby Jesus.

Resources
- 4 large pieces of cardboard or poly board per group of three children
- A selection of different-textured wools
- Masking tape
- Felt
- Fabrics
- Glue

Approach

1. Cut a length of wool and stick in place at the bottom of a board with a piece of masking tape. Wind the wool around the card and use masking tape when the wool has been used up. Continue this process using different colours and textures of wool. Create backgrounds for the three different scenes and one for the roof of the stable.

2. Cut out shapes of the shepherds, kings and so on, from the felt and oddments of fabric, and glue in place.

3. The boards could be taped together in the shape of a stable, the fourth board covered using brown wool for the roof, with nativity figures in the foreground.

4. Alternatively, the boards could be displayed individually to show the story in sequence.

Advent Calendar Display

Advent starts at the beginning of December. Talk to the children about the excitement and anticipation as Christmas approaches. Read the poem below, pointing out the true meaning of Christmas to Christians. Make an Advent display with doors that can be opened each day of the Advent season.

Resources
- Large sheets of different-coloured metallic paper
- Black paper
- Silver pens
- Paint and paintbrushes
- Hexagonal templates
- Stick-on jewels

Approach

1. Draw a back view of the three kings on large sheets of metallic paper.

2. Using paint and stick-on jewels, create designs and patterns on the kings' cloaks and crowns.

3. Draw round the hexagonal templates on black paper, then draw six-point snowflakes with silver pen on each hexagon and cut out.

4. Draw and cut out 25 Christmas symbols using the silver pen on black paper.

5. Cut out 25 doors on the three cloaks and stick one Christmas symbol behind each door.

6. Add the snowflakes and lettering and display as shown.

It's coming to the time of year

It's coming to the time of year
For festive cheer.
It's coming to the time of year
To celebrate with wine and beer.
It's coming to the time of year
To welcome family far and near.
It's coming to the time of year
For cards and toys and joyous noise.
It's coming to the time of year
For cakes and treats and other sweets.
It's coming to the time of year
When the real meaning of Christmas is almost overlooked –
The shepherds in the field
The wise men from afar
Their long intrepid journey
Following a star
A baby in a manger
Their true joy and mirth
It's coming to the time of year
To celebrate His birth.

Valerie Evans

The Yellow Christ, 1889 by Paul Gauguin (1848-1903) © Albright-Knox Art Gallery/CORBIS

The Yellow Christ

Paul Gauguin (1848–1903) painted a triptych of religious paintings in 1889. These were entitled *The Agony in the Garden*, *The Crucifixion* or *The Yellow Christ* and *The Deposition* or *The Green Christ*. Gauguin's *The Yellow Christ* shows the crucifixion in a very personal response to the subject. Like other post-impressionists, Gauguin has expressed his feelings through bright colours and free brushwork, and the yellow Christ on the cross dominates the picture. In the painting, the figures around the cross are dressed in the costume of the painter's own time, and ordinary life is shown to go on with a small Breton figure climbing over a wall in the background. The local landscape used is Pont-Aven in Brittany where Gauguin lived in the 1880s.

Yellow Christ Display

Many Christians regard Easter Sunday as the most important festival in the Christian calendar. During Holy Week, all the events in the last week of Jesus' life are remembered. On Palm Sunday, Jesus rode into Jerusalem on a donkey amidst great celebrations. On Maundy Thursday, Jesus shared a meal of bread and wine with his disciples just before his arrest and death; this is known as the Last Supper. Today, the ceremony of Holy Communion, in which the worshippers receive bread and wine, is a reminder of this event. Jesus was put to death, or crucified, on Good Friday. On Easter Sunday, Jesus rose from the dead, and this gives Christians their most important day of remembrance and celebration.

Look at *The Yellow Christ* (see page 14) and talk about how the colours affect the mood of the painting. Discuss the feelings that Jesus' followers must have experienced at the time of the crucifixion. Paint the crucifixion, inspired by Gauguin, using a limited palette on an aluminium foil background.

Resources
- Cardboard
- Aluminium foil
- Poster paints and paintbrushes
- Masking tape

Approach

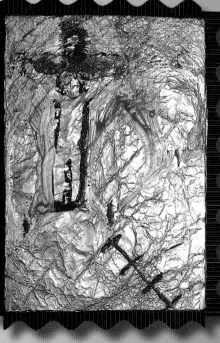

1. Scrunch up a piece of aluminium foil that is slightly larger than the cardboard and then flatten out by hand.

2. Divide the class into four groups, each one working with a different colour palette, for example, 'The Blue Christ', 'The Purple Christ' and so on. Fold the aluminium foil around the cardboard and then paint the crucifixion scene as inspired by Gauguin's work.

3. Make palm crosses from folded masking tape and display.

Beliefs

Hinduism is the main religion of India and one of the oldest religions in the world. Hindus believe in one supreme god, Brahman, who is worshipped in many different forms as gods and goddesses.

The god Shiva is said to dance to destroy ignorance and create understanding. He is often depicted with snakes around his body, and with three eyes so that he can look at the past, the present and the future. He is married to Durga, the mother goddess, who has five pairs of arms and many sides to her character. She can change from loving and caring to angry and frightening.

Lakshmi is the goddess of wealth, remembered at the Divali festival celebrated in autumn. Houses are decorated with lights and flowers so that Lakshmi will want to visit.

People who worship Vishnu believe that he and his wife Lakshmi can appear on Earth in different forms; Rama and Sita are forms of Vishnu and Lakshmi.

Krishna is one of the most popular gods. He is remembered at the festival of Holi and is usually depicted with bluish skin, the colour associated with holiness.

Ganesha, the elephant-headed son of Shiva, is the god who will help to bring success. Hindus pray to Ganesha when they begin a new job or start at a new school.

Gods and Goddesses Display

Make stick shadow puppets from cardboard to show some of the different Hindu gods and display around a central painting of Durga. The puppets can be used to tell stories of the gods.

Resources
- A4 thin card
- Felt-tipped pens
- Split pins
- Paints and paintbrushes
- Masking tape
- Wooden sticks
- Gold and silver doilies

Approach

1. Draw the different gods on A4 thin card with separate limbs, which can be joined as movable parts to the main body with split pins.

2. Ganesha should have two heads, with the elephant head joined to the neck with a split pin so that it can be moved to reveal the human head.

3. Colour or paint the puppets, cut them out and join all the movable parts using split pins. Use masking tape to join each puppet onto a wooden stick.

4. Paint a cut-out figure of Durga with her five pairs of arms. Add gold and silver doilies to decorate her dress and create bracelets around her many arms.

16

The Wheel of Life

The following was written in the Bhagavad Gita – the most important Hindu religious text.

> Certain is death for all those born and certain is birth for all those dead.
> Therefore over the inevitable you should not grieve.
>
> *Bhagavad Gita 2, 27*

Hindus believe that over millions of years the universe is created, exists and is then destroyed, before being created once again. In the same way, living things are trapped in an endless cycle of life, death and rebirth. This cycle is known as Samsara and is symbolised as a wheel, known as the wheel of life. The wheel of life is kept spinning by a power known as karma. Karma refers to the actions of an individual during a lifetime. A good action improves the chances of a better rebirth. Being born again and again on Earth is called reincarnation and Hindus believe that it is possible for a human being to be reborn as an animal. Most Hindus are vegetarian, as they believe all creatures are simply at a different stage in the struggle towards a better life. Hindus respect all animals, but cows and bulls are shown a special reverence because of their usefulness in everyday life. Cows are decorated with painted horns, balloons and streamers at festivals to give thanks for the food and the help with labour that they give to people.

Festival Cows

Approach

1. Draw large cows' heads with horns on cardboard and then turn into 3-D heads by adding papier mâché pulp. Allow the pulp to dry and harden.

2. Paint the cows' heads, adding colourful horns using red and gold ribbon. Decorate the cows with streamers and other collage materials.

3. Draw the symbol for the wheel of life on paper, paint gold and cut out.

4. Display the cows and the circle of life with balloons and streamers. The quote from the Bhagavad Gita could also be added to the display.

Resources
- Paints and paintbrushes
- Papier mâché
- Collage materials
- Streamers
- Balloons
- Cardboard
- Thick black felt-tipped pens
- Gold paint
- Red and gold ribbon

Places of Worship

Hindus worship in temples called mandirs. These temples vary greatly – some are huge and very ornate in design, others are small and simple. Some temples are covered with intricate carvings of demons, gods, humans and animals. Each temple is home to a particular god, where the priest looks after the image of the god, dressing it in fine clothes and making offerings of food. When Hindus visit a mandir they remove their shoes and women cover their heads with their saris as a sign of respect for the god. As part of their worship, Hindus walk in a clockwise direction around the main shrine where there is a sacred image, called a murti, of a Hindu god. Sacred images of other deities stand in smaller shrines on each side. When Hindus leave the mandir they are given prashad. Prashad is food that has been offered to the god.

Hindu Mandir

As a class, make a large, ornate mandir covered with carvings of demons, gods, people and animals.

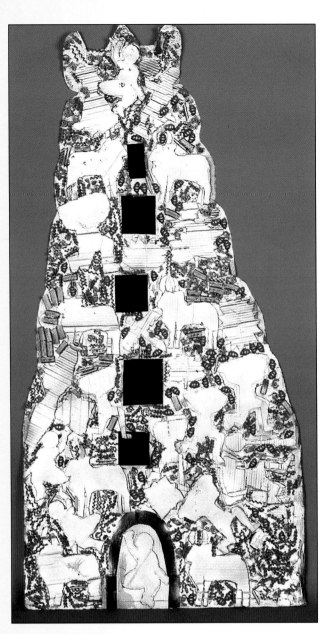

Resources
- Cardboard
- PVA glue
- Gold or silver spray-paint
- Pasta
- Black paper

Approach

1. Draw on cardboard and then cut out an image suitable for the decoration of a mandir, for example, a boy playing a flute, a lotus flower, a lamp and so on.

2. Re-draw the image several times on cardboard, making each image slightly smaller than the last.

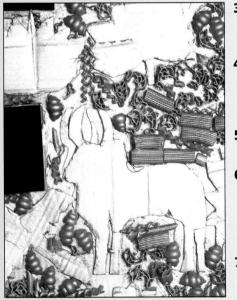

3. Use PVA glue to stick the images one on top of the other to create a 3-D effect.

4. Cover a large cardboard outline of a mandir (at least 1.5m in height) with the images.

5. Fill in any gaps with different-shaped pasta.

6. Spray the mandir gold or silver. It could be displayed with a sign created using the same layering technique.

7. Add black paper to show windows and a door frame.

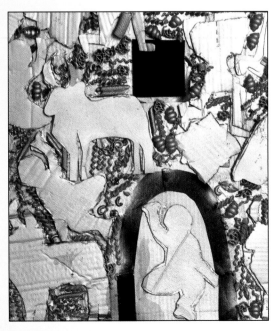

Ganesha Shrine

The shrine in a Hindu home might be a simple cupboard, a shelf or even a small room. The most important item in the shrine is the murti, the image of a god or goddess. The god must be surrounded by beautiful objects and smells, and so flowers and perfumes are always part of the shrine. Near the shrine is a small bell which is rung before prayers or puja, another name for worship. An arti lamp is offered to the murti. The lamp has five flames to represent the five elements (air, earth, fire, water and ether). The person worshipping passes his or her hands over the flame and also over their head. They pray that life will be good in the days to come.

Make a small shrine in the classroom to honour a god or goddess. The shrine shown here is devoted to the elephant-headed god, Ganesha.

Resources
- Clay and clay tools
- A selection of different-coloured tissue paper
- Silver paper
- Fabric
- Paints and paintbrushes
- PVA glue
- Cardboard box
- Varnish
- Flowers, fruit, incense sticks and candles to decorate the shrine

Approach

1. Open up a cardboard box and cut away one side to leave three sides.

2. Draw a picture of the Hindu god Ganesha in the middle section.

3. Scrunch small pieces of torn tissue paper and use to cover the different areas of the design. Decorate the two remaining sides with silver paper and fabric.

4. Make small clay models of Ganesha, allow to dry and harden. Paint and varnish the clay models.

5. Display the Ganesha picture with the clay models. The children could also add flowers, fruit, incense sticks and candles to the shrine.

6. A Hindu prayer, such as the one below, could be displayed near the shrine.

Goodness
Goodness, love, grace and gentleness,
Courtesy, friendship and modesty,
Honesty, penance and chastity, charity
Respect, reverence and truthfulness,
Purity and self-control, wisdom and worship –
All these together are perfect virtue,
And are the words of the loving Lord.

⚠ **Note:** Ensure safety when lighting candles and incense sticks.

Stories and Paintings

Vishnu Reclining on the Serpent Sesha, Attended by Lakshmi and Watched Over by Siva and Parvati, with Nandi, the Bull Mount of Siva (paint on paper), Indian School, (18th Century)/Private Collection, Ann & Bury Peerless Picture Library/ www.bridgeman.co.uk

Vishnu and Sesha

This eighteenth-century painting is based on a Hindu creation myth. According to the Hindu story, before the creation of the Universe, nothing existed except Vishnu, who slept on the thousand-headed serpent Sesha, while floating on the sea of eternity. The god, Brahma, sprang from Vishnu's navel onto a lotus flower and created the world. The goddess, Lakshmi, who is the goddess of good fortune, is shown in the painting rubbing Vishnu's feet. Both Vishnu and Brahma are shown with four arms, implying they have more powers than humans. Also in the painting are Parvati and Shiva with Nandi the bull.

A Hindu Painting

Look at the painting on page 20 and use it to inspire your class to work together to make a large collage display. Create a mixed-media painting based on this work.

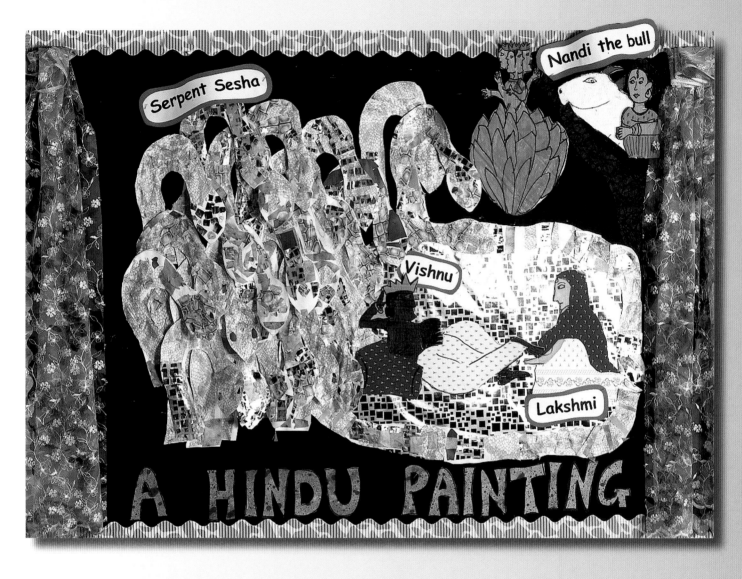

Approach

1. Draw individual snake heads on cardboard, cut them out and decorate with collage paper.

2. Draw pictures of Vishnu resting, Lakshmi kneeling rubbing Vishnu's feet and Brahma emerging from a lotus flower. Decorate the figures using wallpaper samples, fabrics, stick-on jewels and beads.

3. Paint Nandi, the white bull, and create Shiva from collage materials.

4. Join all the snakes to make one many-headed snake, floating on the sea of eternity. Add the other characters to the display.

5. Make labels for the characters shown in the painting.

Resources
- Paints and paintbrushes
- Fabrics
- Cardboard
- Beads
- Wallpaper samples
- Stick-on jewels
- Collage materials
- Collage paper
- A4 white paper

The Rescue of Sita

The story of Rama and his wife Sita comes from the holy book, *Ramayana*, and it is popular with Hindus everywhere. The *Ramayana* is a dramatic poem with some 96 000 verses, covering Rama's life story from his childhood to his rule as a popular king. The *Ramayana* is full of exciting and gripping adventures dealing with themes such as love and deception, war and peace and good over evil, as illustrated in the story of Rama overcoming the evil demon Ravana on page 23.

Read the story on the opposite page to the class. Paint ceramic tiles to illustrate the story of Sita's rescue from Ravana.

Resources
- Ceramic tiles that have been 'biscuit' fired
- Ceramic paints and paintbrushes
- Use of a kiln for final firing

Approach

1. Draw a design onto a tile showing Rama, Sita, Lakshmana, Hanuman, Ravana, or monkeys with the bridge in the background.

2. Paint the design with ceramic paints.

3. If it is necessary to repaint over certain areas of colour, allow 5–10 minutes drying time before doing so.

4. Fire the tiles in a kiln under the supervision of a teacher.

5. The tiles could be displayed in story sequence.

The Rescue of Princess Sita

Prince Rama was the eldest son and heir of King Dasharatha, but instead of ruling the kingdom, Rama and his wife Sita were exiled and lived in a forest rather than a palace.

One day, when Rama was out hunting with his brother Lakshmana, Sita was kidnapped by Ravana, a demon with ten heads, and taken to the island of Lanka.

Lakshmana and the monkey god, Hanuman, helped Rama to track Ravana down on the island. Many monkeys, loyal to Hanuman, helped to build a great bridge across to the island and a fierce battle took place.

During the battle, Lakshmana was seriously wounded and it was left to Hanuman to find the herbs that were needed for his recovery.

Hanuman found a mountain where the herbs grew but, not knowing which to take, he uprooted the whole mountain and took it back to the island and Lakshmana was cured.

In the final battle, Rama killed the many-headed demon Ravana, and Sita was rescued. Rama, Sita, Lakshmana and Hanuman returned home in a flying carriage – their exile and their ordeal over.

Festivals and Ceremonies

The festival of Makar Sankranti is a colourful celebration, considered to be a day of good fortune when bonfires are lit and beautiful kites are flown in competitions. Makar Sankranti takes place in January and is celebrated as a harvest festival when Hindus give thanks for the fertility of the soil.

Makar Sankranti

Approach

1. Draw a flying bird shape on card and cut it out. Tear off enough aluminium foil to easily cover the bird and gently scrunch up by hand.

2. Flatten the foil and then use it to cover the bird, folding it neatly around the edges. Cover the bird with small pieces of torn tissue paper and spread glue on top of the tissue pieces to make sure that they are all flat.

3. Sprinkle sequins onto the bird kite.

4. Create a bonfire by drawing with wax crayons on cut-out flames and then painting over them with drawing inks. Add small twigs collected from the school grounds.

5. Add strings to each kite and display them flying around the bonfire.

6. Use the fluorescent paints to paint fireworks in the sky on the display background.

Resources
- Card
- Aluminium foil
- Tissue paper
- PVA glue
- Sequins
- Twigs and small branches
- Wool or string
- Thin card
- Brown and black wax crayons
- Yellow, red and orange drawing inks
- Fluorescent paints and paintbrushes

Navaratri and Dassehra

Navaratri and Dassehra celebrations are held across India in October and celebrate the triumph of good over evil. 'Navaratri' means 'nine nights' and 'Dassehra' means 'tenth day', and together they make up the ten-day festival that celebrates Durga, the mother goddess. In eastern India the festival celebrates the victory of Durga over the buffalo demon who wanted to destroy the world.

Durga and her army marched to slay the buffalo demon called Mahisha. Mahisha had also had his own army before Durga's followers destroyed it. Mahisha became so angered that he attacked the lion on which Durga was riding, using his sharp horns, and then he escaped Durga's lasso by changing into a lion himself. Durga sliced off his head using her sharp sword but the demon then became a man. Durga then tried to shoot him with arrows but he turned into an elephant. When she cut off the elephant's trunk he became a buffalo once again and Durga was finally able to kill him. She celebrated her victory of good over evil.

As a class, make oil pastel drawings to tell the story of Durga fighting the buffalo demon, Mahisha. Each group can be given a story line to illustrate:

- Durga, with her five pairs of arms carrying weapons, riding on the back of a lion.
- The buffalo demon, Mahisha, attacking Durga with his horns.
- Durga with her lasso trying to capture Mahisha as a lion and slicing off his head.
- Durga on her lion fighting Mahisha as a man.
- Durga fighting Mahisha as an elephant and slicing off his trunk.
- Durga killing the buffalo demon.

Approach

1. Give each group a storyline to illustrate on white poly board.

2. Outline the design with black outliner.

3. Colour the design using oil pastels or felt-tipped pens.

4. Mount the poly boards on small cardboard boxes. Cover the boxes with black paper and display the story in sequence.

Resources
- White poly board
- Black outliner pens
- Oil pastels or felt-tipped pens
- Small cardboard boxes
- Black paper

Beliefs

Sikhism began in India in the fifteenth century. Sikhs follow the teachings of Gurus (religious teachers). There were ten very important Gurus – the first of whom was called Guru Nanak. After the tenth Guru, it was decided there wouldn't be any more human Gurus. Instead, Sikhs would follow the Guru Granth Sahib, a holy book.

Sikhs believe that God is eternal. They believe that he made the universe and everything in it and only one god should be worshipped. The word 'Sikh' means 'disciple' and comes from the Punjabi language. God is known by two different names – Satnam, meaning 'eternal reality', and Raheguru, which means 'wonderful Lord'. In late November or early December, Sikhs celebrate the birthday of Guru Nanak – the founder of their religion. After reading from the Guru Granth Sahib, everyone eats a meal from the same bowl as a symbol that all Sikhs are equal before God. *Mela* by Jean Kenward on page 27 describes this celebration.

Ten Gurus

Make a gallery of portraits showing the ten Gurus, adding beads and stick-on jewels to enhance the finished work. Display each painting in an ornate gold or silver frame.

Resources
- Oil pastels
- White paper
- Gold doilies
- Beads
- Coloured wool
- Gold foil
- Small pegs
- 2 foil platters
- Pencils
- Ballpoint pens
- Stick-on jewels

Approach

1. Draw the first and the last guru with pencil on white paper cut to the size of the middle of the foil platters.

2. Draw the other eight gurus on white paper cut to the size of the middle of the gold doilies.

3. Use oil pastels to colour in the pictures of the ten gurus.

4. Using PVA glue, stick the completed pictures on the doilies and platters and decorate the platters with beads and stick-on jewels.

5. Cut out lettering for the display from gold foil and decorate with patterns on the reverse using a ballpoint pen to create an embossed effect.

6. Using small pegs, hang the letters from coloured wool as shown in the display.

Mela

Listen to the reading,
listen to the hymn.
Today it is a holy day.
Let us think of him
who guided us
and brought us
from darkness
into light –
into sudden morning
out of thick night.

Let us eat together.
Let us take our ease.
Let us throw our weapons down.
Here, is peace.

Jean Kenward

© Belair

The Five Ks

The tenth Guru, Guru Gobind Singh, founded the Sikh community, the Khalsa. Guru Gobind Singh gave the brotherhood a distinct uniform with five items all beginning with the letter K and therefore known as the five Ks. These are the kesh, the kangha, the kachera, the kara and the kirpan. 'Kesh' means 'uncut hair', which is kept tidy with a turban or, in the case of boys too young to join the Khalsa, a small cloth. To keep their long hair tidy a kangha (wooden comb) is used. White shorts called kachera are worn under clothes and symbolise modesty and purity. The kara is a steel bangle worn on the right arm as a reminder to fight only for God. The kirpan is a short sword – a reminder to defend the truth. Many Sikhs today wear a brooch of the kirpan instead of carrying a sword.

Approach

1. Draw around a child and paint on the clothes to show a member of the Sikh brotherhood.

2. Add a bamboo cane with a fabric Sikh flag fixed to the top and attach it to the figure's hand as shown.

3. Draw and cut out pictures showing the kesh, the kangha, the kachera, the kara and the kirpan and stick into the middle of each silver plate. Attach these around the figure with labels.

4. Using 3-D paints, write the title 'The 5 Ks' on small, round cork mats and decorate with sequins and then place on yellow paper circles for the title of the display.

Resources
- White sugar paper
- Paints and paintbrushes
- Selection of fabrics
- PVA glue
- Circular cork mats
- 10 small silver plates
- 5 yellow paper circles
- 3-D paints
- Bamboo cane
- Sequins

Places of Worship

Sikhs give praise to God in their place of worship, the gurdwara, on any day of the week. Gurdwaras can be recognised by the flag which flies above the building. It is yellow with the Sikh symbol on it and it is called the Nishan Sahib.

Before entering the worship room, Sikhs take off their shoes and they may wash their hands and feet. Men either wear a turban or cover their head before entering and usually sit on the opposite side of the room to the women. Everybody sits on the floor to show

equality and nobody turns their back on the Guru Granth Sahib, as they feel that being in the presence of their holy book is like being in front of God. At the service a chauri is waved over the Guru Granth Sahib. The chauri is a special fan made from hair or feathers. During worship, readings are given, hymns are sung and the service ends with the Ardas, a special prayer to remember God and the ten Gurus. The Mool Mantar prayer shown below begins the Guru Granth Sahib. It was composed by the first Guru, Guru Nanak.

Holy Book and Fan

Approach

1. Open the book and place it on top of the cardboard box.

2. Put water into the tray or bowl and soak small strips of modroc for 2–3 seconds before using to cover the book and the box. Cover completely and then allow to dry.

3. Paint a yellow and red patterned border to the pages of the book and then use a black felt-tipped pen to copy part of one of the Sikh hymns in the early Sikh script.

4. Cover the box with colourful fabric.

5. To make a chauri, attach peacock feathers to a short bamboo stick using masking tape. Paint the masking tape and the bamboo stick with gold paint.

Resources

- Large cardboard box
- Water tray or bowl of water
- Large, old book that is no longer used
- Modroc
- Colourful fabric
- Short bamboo stick
- Peacock feathers
- Masking tape
- Black felt-tipped pens
- Gold, red and yellow paints and paintbrushes

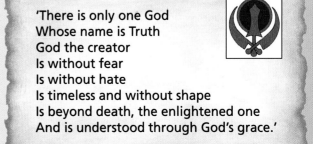

'There is only one God
Whose name is Truth
God the creator
Is without fear
Is without hate
Is timeless and without shape
Is beyond death, the enlightened one
And is understood through God's grace.'

Stories and Paintings

Mss.Panj.B.40 f.123 *Guru Nanak and King Shivanabh*, 1773. By permission of the British Library.

Guru Nanak was born into a Hindu family near Lahore in modern-day Pakistan. He knew many Muslims, but he was not satisfied by either Hinduism or Islam and he decided to follow a path of God on which everyone is regarded as equal whatever their religion, colour or sex. The followers of Guru Nanak became known as Sikhs (disciples) and he taught fellow Sikhs to work to earn an honest living, share food with others and to be helpful and charitable. He chose two helpers who appear sitting next to him in many Sikh paintings. One was a Hindu called Bala and the other was a Muslim musician called Mardana who composed some of the music for Guru Nanak's songs, which are still sung in the gurdwara on Guru Nanak's birthday.

Guru Nanak

Look at the painting on page 30 with the children and discuss what is happening in the image and the characters shown. Create a 3-D painting of Guru Nanak with his helper, Mardana, using this painting for inspiration.

Approach

1. Paint the base of the cardboard box blue and black for the background of the scene and paint the surround of the box in red.

2. Paint the figures on card showing Mardana holding rubab, his musical instrument, and Bala with his hands clasped. Cut out the figures.

3. Using the wooden end of a small paintbrush, add dots to the background scene to represent the flowers and shrubs.

4. Draw and paint a separate white arch to add to the front of the red surround as a gateway.

5. Paint white birds flying in the sky.

6. Using adhesive squares, stick the figures to the background to give them a slightly raised effect.

Resources
- Cardboard box
- Additional cardboard
- Adhesive squares
- Paints and paintbrushes

Guru Har Gobind and the 52 Princes

At the time of Guru Har Gobind, the sixth Guru, India was ruled by the Emperor Jahangir. The emperor was a devout Muslim and didn't like the popularity of the Sikh religion. He invited Guru Har Gobind on a hunting trip to find out about the army that the Guru was training. Whilst on this trip, Guru Har Gobind saved the emperor's life when a tiger leapt out to attack him, making them good friends.

When the emperor became ill, his astrologers told him that he would only get better if he asked a holy man to go to the fort at Gwalior to pray for his recovery. The astrologers wanted Guru Har Gobind out of the way, and Gwalior was, after all, a prison. However, when the emperor was well again he told the Guru that he was free to go but Guru Har Gobind refused to leave prison unless 52 Hindu princes were released with him. He was told to leave through a narrow gate and all those who could hold onto his cloak could have their freedom. Guru Har Gobind fastened long cords to his cloak so that the 52 princes could leave with him.

When Guru Har Gobind returned home to Amritsar after his release from Gwalior Fort, Sikhs decorated the Golden Temple with lights to welcome him back. Every year at Divali the Golden Temple is illuminated and there are fireworks to remember his homecoming. Sikh homes are decorated with oil lamps (called divas), candles and coloured lights. People give sweets to their friends and relatives and there are special meals. It is a happy, colourful celebration.

Divali

'Divali' means 'festival of lights'. At Divali, Sikhs remember when the sixth Guru, Guru Har Gobind, was released from prison and everyone in Amritsar lit lamps in their windows to welcome him home. The Golden Temple at Amritsar is built on a large platform in the middle of an artificial lake. The water of the temple is believed to be very holy, like amrit, the sacred drink of the Sikhs, and that is why the city is called Amritsar. The temple has four entrances and is built in marble with the top half covered in gold leaf. Verses from the Guru Granth Sahib are carved on the temple walls, and readings from the Sikhs' holy book begin at dawn and continue into the evening.

Read the story on page 32 with the class and make a display of the Golden Temple at night surrounded by Guru Har Gobind and the 52 princes.

Approach

Resources
- White paper
- Paintbrushes
- Oil pastels
- 3-D yellow paint
- 3-D gold and blue pens
- Stick-on stars
- Coloured wool
- Black and gold paint

1. Draw the Golden Temple with its reflection on white paper. Outline the temple with yellow 3-D paint to give a raised effect.

2. Paint the temple gold and the night sky black. Add stick-on stars to the night sky.

3. Paint lights on the temple using a 3-D gold pen and add detail with the 3-D blue pen.

4. Draw Guru Har Gobind and the 52 princes on white paper and colour using oil pastels.

5. Display the temple in the centre of a board and put the princes around the edges attached to the Guru's cloak by lengths of coloured wool.

Festivals and Ceremonies

Sikhs celebrate two sorts of festivals – gurpurbs and melas. Gurpurbs remember the birth or death of one of the gurus. Melas are fairs and are similar to Hindu festivals.

Baisakhi

The festival of Baisakhi includes the Sikh New Year and was the occasion when Guru Gobind Singh founded the Khalsa (the Sikh community). During Baisakhi, there are celebrations at the gurdwara all day and people eat the langar, a special meal that is part of Sikh worship. There are processions with the Sikh holy book carried on an open vehicle for all to see. Hymns are sung in celebration. At Baisakhi, groups of men perform original bhangra dancing – a kind of folk dancing that began in the Punjab, India. The bhangra dance is performed at the end of the harvest and tells the story of the farmer's life. They begin the dance by carrying their tools to the field and keep looking up at the sky in the hope of rain. When the rain comes, the dancers weed and cut the crop and finally go off to the fair to celebrate. The dance is accompanied by the voice of a solo singer and a big, barrel-shaped two-ended drum called a dhol. The dancers wear colourful costumes and headdresses to perform the bhangra dance.

Approach

1. Draw the bhangra dancers in different dancing positions on thin card.

2. Use the material to dress the dancers in long red robes, white tunics and gold waistcoats edged with patterned braid.

3. Cut out the gold doilies into a fan shape and add a band of braid. Stick onto the heads of the figures as decorative headdresses.

4. Add hair and facial features using felt-tipped pens and wool.

5. Add bead necklaces to the figures.

Resources
- Large pieces of thin card
- Gold, red and white fabrics
- Patterned braid
- Gold doilies
- Black and brown wool
- Beads
- PVA glue
- Sequins
- Felt-tipped pens

Marriage

Sikh marriage is called Anand karaj, which means 'the ceremony of bliss'. It takes place in front of the Guru Granth Sahib to show that the couple are seeking the grace and blessing of God on their marriage. The couple are asked to be faithful to one another, to celebrate each other's joys and to help each other through sorrow and pain. They are also asked to show respect and kindness to their relatives. Their marriage agreement is shown when they bow before the Guru Granth Sahib. At the ceremony, a hymn called the lavan is spoken and then sung – each of the four verses explains a different stage of life. As each verse is sung, the couple walk in a clockwise direction around the Guru Granth Sahib four times. The couple are joined together by a pink scarf, which the bridegroom wears at the start of the ceremony. He also wears a red turban and a kalgri (face mask). The guests often throw flower petals over the couple. At the end of the marriage ceremony the blessed food, karah parshad, is shared with the congregation.

Approach

1. Draw the head and shoulders of the Sikh bride and groom.

2. Colour the faces using wax crayons. Add white material for the groom's suit and deep red for his turban.

3. Make a kalgri (face mask) from gold card and decorate with gold and silver sequins. Hang lengths of gold and silver tinsel from the mask. Stick the mask in place.

4. Add fabric for the bride's kameez. This is a long, beautifully embroidered tunic. Display as shown with flower petals around the Sikh bride and groom.

Resources
- Wax crayons
- PVA glue
- Red and white fabric
- Gold card
- Gold and silver tinsel
- Gold and silver sequins
- Poly board or cardboard
- Doilies

Beliefs

The founder of Buddhism was Siddattha Gotama (now known as the Buddha). He lived a very privileged but sheltered life. Although he wanted for nothing, this did not make him content. One day, Siddattha asked Channa, his charioteer, to take him out for a ride. He was shocked to see an old man, then a sick man and finally a dead man. Until then he had been unaware of suffering in the world. He then met a monk who had no possessions but nevertheless seemed contented.
Siddattha then decided to leave his wife and child and all the comforts of the palace to live like the monk. He fasted and prayed for many years before finding the answers that he had been looking for. He finally understood the basic truths of life and achieved enlightenment. At the centre of his first sermon were the Four Noble Truths, which are:

1. Human life is full of suffering.
2. The cause of suffering is greed.
3. There is an end to suffering.
4. The way to end suffering is to follow the Noble Eightfold Path.

The Noble Eightfold Path lies somewhere between extreme luxury and extreme hardship and it is a complete way of life that Buddhists try to follow today.

The Buddha Passing Away

When the Buddha died, Buddhists believe that he entered nirvana – the blissful state that is seen by Buddhists as an end to all suffering. They believe that people are reborn many times before they reach nirvana. In daily life, Buddhists follow guidelines called the five precepts. These five precepts are: do not harm or kill living things, do not take things unless they are freely given, lead a decent life, do not speak unkindly or tell lies, and do not drink alcohol or take drugs. In living a good life and following these guidelines, Buddhists hope to build up merit to improve their next rebirth.

Resources
- Red paper
- Black felt-tipped pens
- Cardboard
- 3-D gold pens
- Gold and red paint and paintbrushes
- Orange fabric
- Wool
- Ribbon
- Hole punch
- Card foot template

Approach

1. Cut five oval hoops from cardboard and wind strips of orange fabric around each hoop. Draw five different Buddhas – one to fit inside each hoop.
2. Outline each Buddha with 3-D gold pens and then paint gold.
3. Using a hole punch, make a hole in the top of each Buddha and hang from wool inside the hoop.
4. Draw the Buddha lying in the reclining position using black felt-tipped pens on red paper. Add designs to the robe using 3-D gold pens and display as shown.
5. Use the card foot template to print footprints on the ribbon for the top and bottom of the border.

Clay Buddha

Depictions of the Buddha vary greatly depending on when and where they were made, but all aim to convey the sense of high esteem in which the Buddha is held. In all statues, the Buddha is shown with half-closed eyes, looking very serene. In Thailand, the Buddha is often shown making the Earth-witnessing gesture in which the right hand is turned towards the ground. The Thai Buddha often has a tightly curled hairstyle, pointed headdress and fine features. The flame-like headdress represents the light of supreme knowledge. Sometimes the Buddha is shown in the cross-legged, half-lotus, meditating position. Meditation is a way of training and calming the mind. Buddhists believe that meditating will bring them closer to enlightenment. The Japanese Buddha is often depicted in the meditating position, in which the palms of the hands face upwards and the fingers and thumbs touch at the tips. Sometimes the Buddha is depicted standing, dancing or reclining, which is said to show his death posture.

Using clay, create different models of Buddha, making sure that the children include the features common to all Buddhas, for example, serene features.

Approach

1. Using clay, model different-style Buddhas – some standing, some meditating and some reclining – taking care when modelling the position of the hands.

2. Use clay tools to show patterning, for example, the flow of robes and so on.

3. Instead of modelling an elaborate headdress, model the Buddha's head and then push a small pine cone into the head as an ornate headdress.

4. Add stick-on jewels to the edging of the Buddha's robes.

5. Allow the models to dry and harden and then paint gold.

Resources
- Clay
- Clay tools
- Small pine cones
- Stick-on jewels
- Gold paint and paintbrushes

Places of Worship

Some Buddhist temples are very simple, unadorned shrines, while others are huge structures with complex carvings and beautiful paintings. Above one of the entrances to the Baiju Temple in Tibet there is a mural of the Buddha's eyes with the urna, sometimes called a beauty spot or a wisdom eye, between them. The eyes are ever watchful of those entering and leaving the temple. All Buddhist temples, however grand or simple, contain statues of the Buddha and provide a place where Buddhists can gather to reflect, make offerings and meditate. At the start of the new year, brightly-coloured prayer flags flutter from temples and monasteries and also homes. Each flutter of the flags is regarded as a repetition of the prayer that is written on it and the wind carries the prayers into the world.

A Buddhist Temple

Create a display showing part of a temple decorated with the Buddha's eyes and lots of brightly-coloured flags tied to lengths of wool. Ask the children to write a simple prayer of their own to add to each flag.

Approach

1. Draw an outline of the top part of the temple on silver collage paper and cut out.

2. Cut rectangular flags from the brightly-coloured A4 paper.

3. On white paper, make a collage of the Buddha's eyes using black and gold felt-tipped pens, paper mosaic tiles and 3-D paints.

Resources
- White paper
- Paper mosaic tiles
- 3-D paints and paintbrushes
- Gold and black felt-tipped pens
- Wool
- Tissue paper
- A4 brightly-coloured paper
- Gold metallic paper
- Silver collage paper
- Thin card
- Stapler

4. Display the Buddha's eyes as part of the temple design.

5. Attach wool, running from the top of the temple to underneath the Buddha's eyes, and tie the brightly-coloured prayer flags to these. Cover a rectangle of thin card with gold metallic paper and staple these to form a cylindrical shape. Add a gold metallic paper fringe and a small spire to the top of the temple to complete the display.

Buddhist Symbols

Lotus flowers are an important symbol for Buddhists. The flowers turn towards the Sun just as Buddhists turn towards knowledge. The Buddha is often shown sitting on a throne of lotus flowers and these are also left at Buddhist shrines. The elephant symbol often appears in Buddhist art. Before Siddattha was born, his mother, Queen Maya, dreamt of a white elephant emerging from a dazzling white light, carrying lotus blossoms in its trunk. She was told that her strange dream meant that when she had a son he would grow up to be a very great and good man. The double-headed fish is a Buddhist symbol of fertility.

Make a display showing a variety of Buddhist symbols, such as a large double-headed fish surrounded by smaller fish and elephants.

Approach

1. Fold the black paper in half and draw a fish shape against the fold, which can be cut out to produce a symmetrical image.

2. Use the 3-D paints to draw scales, fins and patterns on the fish. Allow to dry.

3. Fold the A4 white paper in half and draw a fish against the fold. When cut out, decorate using oil pastels. Use this shape as a template for other fish.

4. Draw and cut out two elephants from sandpaper and display as shown.

Resources
- Black paper
- A4 white paper
- Sandpaper
- 3-D paints and paintbrushes
- Oil pastels

Stories, Prayers and Paintings

Read the story on page 41 to the children. Buddhists often try to convey a message using stories and riddles. The moral of the story on the opposite page is that we need to see the full picture in order to understand something properly.

A Mysterious Creature

Make a wall display to depict the story on page 41 and the message that it is trying to convey.

Approach

1. Draw a large elephant and shade using drawing pencils.

2. Use a black felt-tipped pen to draw jigsaw pieces onto the elephant and photocopy several times. Cut two or three copies into individual puzzle pieces.

3. Make labels asking the question, Is it a tree? Is it a snake? and so on, using suitable collage materials. For the label 'Is it a rope?', coil string to decorate the letters.

4. Display the questions surrounded by the puzzle pieces and elephant pictures.

Resources
- Large white paper
- Drawing pencils
- Black felt-tipped pens
- Wooden letter templates
- Collage paper
- PVA glue
- String

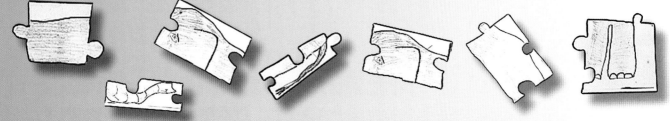

The Blind Men and the Elephant

A strange animal appeared in a land full of blind people and the king sent a team of men to find out what it was. The men were a little scared of touching it while it moved so they waited until it was asleep and perfectly still. The first man felt the elephant's side and declared to the others that it was a wall. The second man felt the elephant's leg and decided it was a large tree. The third man felt the elephant's ear and told the other men that it was a fan. 'It is definitely a snake,' announced the fourth man who was feeling the trunk. The fifth man, who was standing at the other end of the elephant, told the other men that they were all wrong because it was a rope that he was feeling. The blind men were, of course, all feeling the same animal, a large grey elephant!

Together, the blind men could have shared enough information to get to the truth. Buddhism is made up of many different groups who cannot reach the whole truth by themselves, they can only point towards it.

Prayer

Buddhist monks spend their time teaching, praying and meditating. They live simple lives, shave their heads and wear plain clothes. Their belongings might include a needle, a razor, a water strainer and a begging bowl. Meditation is important to all Buddhists and must be done in a comfortable position with a mind clear of all distracting thoughts. It helps to focus on breathing or an object such as a flower or the image of the Buddha. Chanting a series of words over and over again helps to focus the mind during meditation. These words are called a mantra. Many Tibetan Buddhists carry prayer beads to help them count how many times they have repeated a mantra. Prayer beads are usually made from jade, ivory or sandalwood and there are usually 108 beads on the string, which is the number of desires that must be overcome before reaching enlightenment. Tibetan prayer wheels contain a printed mantra on a scroll. The sacred mantra 'Om mani padme hum', meaning 'Hail the jewel in the lotus', is written many times. Spinning the prayer wheel means the mantra is repeated continuously, spreading understanding and well being.

Prayer Wheels and Beads

Resources
- Different-sized cardboard tubes
- Aluminium foil
- Gold 3-D pens
- Blu-tack
- Green plasticine
- String or wool
- White paper
- Paints and paintbrushes

Approach

1. Cover the different-sized cardboard tubes with aluminium foil – two covered tubes for each prayer wheel. The thinner, longer tube acts as the handle.

2. Join the two tubes with Blu-tack.

3. Using a gold 3-D pen, add characters to the top part of the wheel.

4. Make small round beads from green plasticine to represent prayer beads made from jade.

5. Make holes in the beads and thread them onto wool or string.

6. Display the prayer beads and wheels in front of a display board painted to look like the front of a Buddhist temple.

Buddhist Scriptures

The chants or verses sung by the Sangha (Buddhist community) preserve the Buddha's teachings. The Dhammapada is an important scripture which brings together some of the Buddha's sayings. The sayings on this page should promote a great deal of class discussion.

'Better than a thousand useless words is one word that brings peace.'

'The body dies, but the spirit is not placed in a tomb.'

'It is easy to see the faults of others but difficult to see one's own faults. One shows the faults of others like chaff winnowed in the wind but one conceals one's own faults as a cunning gambler conceals his dice.'

All Buddhists try to put aside some time each day to meditate. By meditating regularly every Buddhist hopes to reach nirvana. 'Zen' is a Japanese word, which means 'meditation'. Zen Buddhists use some of the following rather puzzling sentences to aid their meditation.

'Imagine the sound of one hand clapping.'

'What was your true face before your father and mother were born?'

The *Tibetan Book of the Dead* is very important to Buddhists as it helps them to think about the consequences of their present life in order to prepare for the next.

'If you have deserved it a white light will guide you into the heavens and you will have some happiness amongst the gods.'

The Life of Buddha Shakyamuni, detail of his Childhood, Tibetan, 18th century (oil on canvas), NO_DATA/Musee Guimet, Paris, France, Giraudon/www.bridgeman.co.uk

Buddha's First Steps

The man who was to become the Buddha was born Siddattha Gotama in an area of India that is now part of Nepal. He was born in a grove among woods in Lumbini when his mother was on her way to visit family. In some stories it is said that he emerged from his mother's side, was spotlessly clean and was able to walk straight away. A soothsayer visited his home soon after his birth and predicted that he would become a great man. This eighteenth-century Tibetan painting shows the Buddha taking his first steps.

A Buddhist Painting

Statues of the Buddha as a child pointing one hand to Earth and the other to Heaven.

18th century Tibetan painting showing the Buddha's first steps.

As a class, look at the painting on page 44 and discuss the story of the Buddha's birth. Recreate the painting as a display using a variety of materials. Many statues of the young Siddattha show him pointing one hand to Earth and the other to heaven. Use this image on the border of the display.

The first Buddhist shrines were ten dome-shaped mounds, or stupas, which were built to contain the Buddha's ashes. Later, other stupas were built all over the Buddhist world and many now form part of larger temple complexes. When visiting stupas, Buddhists walk around them as a mark of respect to the relics they hold.

Approach

1. Ask ten children to work on individual figures from the painting. Draw the figures on white paper and then add collage materials for the clothing. Use watercolour pencils for the skin and the facial features.

2. Draw, colour and cut out a tree on white paper.

3. Draw and cut out the top part of a stupa.

4. Glue the stupa, the tree and the individual people on the display board, backed with black paper.

5. Use 3-D pens to work directly on the background, adding all the foliage and detail including the fencing.

6. Fold a piece of A4 white paper in half and in half again. Draw the young Siddattha on the front of the folded paper, making sure that both the hand pointing to Earth and the hand pointing to heaven are on the folds.

7. Cut around the figure and open out to show four joined figures.

8. Paint the figures gold, cut as needed and display them around the border.

Resources
- Black backing paper
- Collage materials
- Silver and gold metallic pens
- Watercolour pencils
- Gold paint and paintbrushes
- Red, yellow and gold 3-D pens
- A4 white paper
- PVA glue

Festivals and Ceremonies

At New Year, images of the Buddha are washed and people bathe or are sprayed with water. The idea is that being clean helps Buddhists to start the New Year in a state of spiritual purity. Golden statues of the Buddha are washed by people while others pray or fill water pots for the festival. In Tibet, the New Year festival is called Losar. People dress up in new clothes and eat kapse, which are cakes, as well as other special foods. At the end of the festival, Buddhist monks put on frightening masks to ward off any evil spirits from the previous year.

Resources

- Sketchbooks
- Cardboard
- Papier mâché pulp
- Paints and paintbrushes
- Varnish

New Year Masks

Design and make masks that Tibetan Buddhists could wear at their New Year celebrations.

Approach

1. Produce a mask design in a sketchbook.

2. Draw a copy of the mask onto cardboard and build up the shape of the features with papier mâché pulp. Allow the pulp to dry and harden.

3. Paint the mask using the sketchbook design for reference.

4. Varnish the masks and leave to dry.

Festival of the Tooth

The festival of the Tooth, held in Sri Lanka, lasts for two weeks and is extremely important in uniting the Buddhists and the Hindus who live there. It is predominantly a Buddhist festival, but Hindus join in the celebrations as they believe that the Buddha was an incarnation of the Hindu god, Vishnu. During the festival, the tooth, belonging to the Buddha, is taken from the sacred tooth chamber in a miniature stupa (see page 45) and paraded through the town on a large elephant. The elephant is dressed in embroidered cloth and is followed by hundreds of other richly adorned elephants. The crowd celebrates by throwing flowers in front of the elephants, shouting loudly and blowing conch shells.

Make a parade of elephants dressed in richly decorated fabrics with a painted card stupa on the back of one elephant and people riding or walking by the other elephants.

Resources

- Thin white card
- Elephant templates
- Different-textured fabrics
- Sequins
- Braid
- PVA glue
- Felt-tipped pens (including grey)
- Cocktail umbrellas

Approach

1. Draw around the elephant templates on thin white card and use a grey felt-tipped pen to colour each elephant's trunk and legs.

2. Cover the rest of the elephant with different-textured fabrics, adding braid and sequins.

3. Cut out the elephants and display.

4. Add people riding the elephants or walking beside them. Decorate the people using felt-tipped pens and adding pieces of fabric as required and small cocktail umbrellas as colourful sunshades.

Beliefs

Judaism began with Abraham in about 2000 BCE in the land that we now call Israel. Jews believe in only one God and that he is the creator of all things and that they are God's chosen people because he made a covenant with them when he gave Moses the Ten Commandments. The Jewish holy book, the Torah, teaches that God is the creator, and all that exists comes from God. The Torah is a collection of God's laws, rules and stories.

The Jewish story of the creation tells how God created the world in six days and then rested on the seventh. On the first day, God made light. On the second day, God made the sky full of clouds to hold some of the water from the oceans below. On the third day, God made the land and covered it with flowers, plants and trees. On the fourth day, God added the sun and then the moon and stars to the empty sky. On the fifth day, God filled the sky with birds of every shape, size and colour, and he filled the oceans with fish. The next day, God looked at the empty land and decided to fill it with animals. Finally he made people, and his work was complete. The next day, God rested. The special day for Jews is from Friday evening until Saturday evening and this day is known as Shabbat. It is a day of complete rest, a reminder that God rested on the seventh day after creating the world. Havdalah is the ceremony that marks the end of Shabbat. A spice box is passed around as a symbol of hope for the week ahead. A plaited candle reminds Jewish people that God's first act of creation was to make light.

Creation Tiles

Ask the children to design tiles depicting the creation story.

Approach

1. Make a small concertina book to show pictures of how the world was created. Colour the pictures and give the book a title.

2. Using porcelain outliner pens, copy a favourite design from the book onto one of the tiles.

3. Allow the outline of the design to harden.

4. Fill in the design using porcelain paints and leave to dry for 24 hours.

5. Follow the instructions on the paints and bake the tiles in a low oven (150°C) for 30 minutes. Leave to cool in the oven.

6. Display seven tiles in a row to show the creation story and decorate the border with beads and small mosaic tiles.

Resources
- Paper concertina book with seven pages
- Coloured pencils and felt-tipped pens
- Light-coloured kitchen tiles
- Porcelain paints and paintbrushes
- Beads
- Gold and black porcelain outliner pens
- Mosaic tiles

Shalom

Jews often say 'shalom' instead of 'hello' or 'goodbye' – it means 'peace' in Hebrew. The prophet Isaiah described the age of peace as follows:

The wolf shall live with the lamb.
The leopard with the kid.
The calf and the young lion will be together
and a little child shall lead them.
The cow and the bear shall graze,
Their young shall lie down together;
The lion shall eat straw like the ox.
The nursing child shall play
Over the hole of the asp,
As the weaned child shall put
Its hand on the adder's den.
They will not hurt or destroy on all my
Holy mountain:
For the earth will be full of the knowledge
Of the Lord
As the waters cover the sea.

Isaiah 11, 6–9

Resources
- White paper
- Paints and paintbrushes
- Collage paper
- PVA glue

Approach

1. Give each group of children a different subject to draw and paint:
   a. the wolf with the lamb
   b. the leopard with the kid
   c. the calf and the young lion
   d. the cow grazing with the bear
   e. the lion eating straw with the ox

2. Add collage pieces to the paintings when dry.

3. Mount each painting on a suitably patterned border.

Use Isaiah's words above to help the children understand about bringing opposite sides together and the need for peace in today's world. Create a display showing the different images in Isaiah's description.

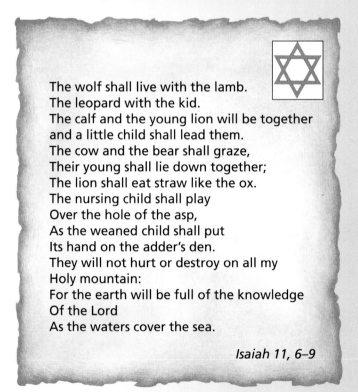

49

Places of Worship

The synagogue is a place where Jews meet to worship God, and is the centre of Jewish life. There are no statues or pictures of God in the synagogue because Jewish people do not believe that God has a body, but that he is the one true God.

Every synagogue has a large cupboard called an Ark, in which the Torah scrolls are kept. The Torah is a collection of Jewish laws, stories and the teachings of God and is the holiest book in Jewish life. The Torah says it is every individual's duty to pursue a good quality of life and to show kindness to strangers. The Ten Commandments are an important part of the Torah and everybody stands when they are read out in the synagogue. The Torah contains over 600 commandments and is written in Hebrew.

Above the Ark is the Ner Tamid or eternal light, which reminds Jews of the seven-branched menorah that used to burn constantly in the Tabernacle, and later in the Temple in Jerusalem. It shows Jewish people that God lives forever.

The Yad

The yad is used by the person reading from the Torah to point to the words to prevent the Torah from being damaged. The end of the yad is sometimes shaped like a hand with a finger pointing. 'Yad' means 'hand' in Hebrew.

Make a yad for pointing to the words in the Torah.

Approach

1. Draw the yad onto cardboard, showing a hand with a finger pointing at the end.

2. Paint the yad silver or gold and add patterns and designs using 3-D paint.

Resources
- Cardboard
- Silver and gold paint and paintbrushes
- Silver, gold and bronze 3-D paint

Jewish Wedding

Bridal casket

Jewish wedding artefacts

Ornate wedding ring

Most Jewish couples marry in a synagogue under a huppah, a cloth canopy supported by four poles. This symbolises the couple's new home and is often decorated with flowers and ribbons. A wedding contract called a ketubah is signed and rings are exchanged. In the past, some Jewish communities would lend the bride an ornate ring often decorated with a miniature house and inscribed with the words 'Mazel Tov', meaning 'good luck'. A highly decorated bridal casket might be given to the bride by the groom. At the end of the ceremony the groom wraps a wine glass in cloth, puts it on the floor and steps on it. This symbolises the fragility of marriage and reminds everyone of the destruction of the Temple.

Design a Jewish bridal casket and an ornate gold ring.

Approach

1. Draw and cut out a casket and gold ring on gold foil using a ballpoint pen. Add an ornate house to the top of the ring and elaborate detail to both ring and casket.

2. Display the ring and the casket reversed to show the embossed design.

Resources
- Gold foil
- Ballpoint pens

Stories and Prayers

Prayer is very important to religious Jewish people. The famous prayer, the Shema, is written on a small parchment scroll and put inside a container called a mezuzah. The mezuzah hangs on the doorposts of a Jewish house. To remind themselves of their faith and the fact that God is always there, family members touch the mezuzah on entering and leaving the house. Mezuzahs can be made of a variety of materials and they are often highly decorated.

Mezuzahs

Design a mezuzah, showing the different Jewish symbols, and display with other Jewish artefacts. Read the words from the Shema on the following page together as a class. Discuss the clothes that Jewish people wear during prayer.

Approach

1. Cut the cardboard to cover the length of the box. Punch a hole in the top of the cardboard – this is for hanging the mezuzah later.

2. Add designs to strips of silver foil and stick these on the boxes or decorate directly onto the cardboard.

3. Enhance the design using 3-D paints.

Resources
- Long, thin boxes
- Cardboard
- Silver foil
- Hole punch
- 3-D paints and paintbrushes
- PVA glue

52

Jewish Scriptures

The Jewish people have many wise sayings such as the following:

'Do not judge a man until you have stood in his place.'

'God gave man one mouth and two ears so that he could listen twice as much as he could speak!'

Judaism is a monotheistic religion, which means that Jews believe in only one God. They feel that they can get closer to God through prayer. Most Jews use a prayer book called a siddur which contains prayers that can be said at home or while praying in the synagogue. For prayer, many Jewish men wear a prayer robe, or tallit, and a kippah and tefillin. The kippah is a cap which can be plain or decorated. Tefillin are small leather boxes which contain the Shema (a famous prayer) written on tiny scrolls. Tefillin are worn on the head and the arm as a sign of the wearer's belief in God.

These words are from the Shema:

'Hear, O Israel, the Lord is our God. The Lord is one. Now you must love your God with all your heart and with all your soul and with all your strength. And these words which I am commanding you today shall be upon your heart ... And you must bind them as a sign upon your arm and they shall be a token between your eyes. And you must write them on the doorposts of your house and on your gates.'

Deuteronomy 6, 4–9

Haman's Pockets

The Book of Esther is called the Megillah, meaning 'scroll'. It is usually read in March when Jews gather in the synagogue to celebrate the festival of Purim. The story of Esther (see page 55) took place hundreds of years ago in a country called Persia, which is now called Iran. Haman hated all Jews and he drew lots to see which day he would murder Mordecai (Esther's cousin) and the other Jews. 'Purim' means 'lots' and this gives the festival its name. In some places, children bake sweet pastries known as hamantaschen or Haman's pockets. They are made from circles of pastry folded to form triangles with a filling of dates, apple, raisins or apricot jam.

Resources

(Makes approximately 12 pastries.)
- Mixing bowl and spoon
- 225g flour
- ¼ teaspoon of baking powder
- Pinch of salt
- 1 egg
- 4 tablespoons of honey
- Melted butter
- Circular pastry cutter
- Fillings – apricot jam, orange marmalade, dates or apple or raisin
- Baking tray

Groggers

Re-read the story of Esther to the children. Design and make groggers.

Approach

Make a honey dough by mixing together 225g flour, ¼ teaspoon of baking powder, a pinch of salt, 1 egg, 4 tablespoons of honey and melted butter. Roll out on a lightly floured board and then, using a circular pastry cutter, cut approximately 12 circles. Choose a filling of either apricot jam, orange marmalade, dates or apple and raisin mixture, adding the filling to the centre of each circle. Fold the edges in to make three corners and bake for 30 minutes at 175°C.

 Note: Some children may be allergic to one or more of the ingredients, so check with guardians for any allergies.

Resources
- Paper plates
- Felt-tipped pens
- Dried peas
- Stapler
- Poly board

Approach

1. Draw pictures, inspired by the story of Esther, on paper plates.

2. Colour the pictures using felt-tipped pens.

3. Staple two paper plates together with dried peas in the middle.

4. Add a decorated handle made from poly board.

Queen Esther

The King of Persia fell in love with Esther and made her his queen, not knowing that she was Jewish. Haman, who helped the king to run the country, hated all Jews and told many lies about them, saying that they didn't obey the king's laws. He gave orders for all the Jews to be killed. Esther's cousin, Mordecai, heard this news and begged Queen Esther for help. Queen Esther arranged a banquet and invited Haman to attend. At the banquet she told the king that she was Jewish and that her people were in danger because of Haman's plans. The King immediately ordered Haman's death and Mordecai became his chief minister.

Jewish people remember brave Queen Esther and celebrate at the feast of Purim. When this story is read out in the synagogue the children hiss, shout, whistle, stamp their feet and shake rattles called groggers every time they hear the evil Haman's name.

Festivals and Ceremonies

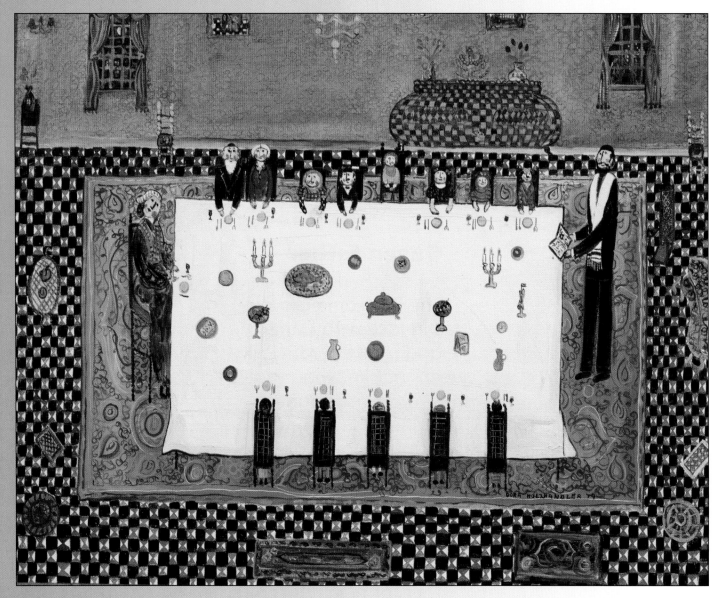

The Passover Meal, Holzhandler, Dora (Contemporary Artist)/RONA Gallery, London, UK/www.bridgeman.co.uk

Passover

Pesach, or Passover, is one of the most important Jewish festivals, when Jewish people remember how Moses led them to freedom after they had been slaves in Egypt. During the eight-day festival, the main celebration is the Seder – the Passover meal at which many of the foods eaten have a special meaning. Lamb on the bone is eaten as a reminder of the lambs killed in Egypt, a hard boiled egg is a symbol of new life, bitter herbs such as horseradish evoke the bitterness of slavery and charoset, a sweet paste made from nuts, cinnamon and apples is a reminder of the sweetness of freedom. The mixture looks rather unappetizing and is supposed to look like the mortar that the Israelites used to build the houses and palaces of Egypt. A green vegetable, usually parsley or lettuce, reminds the Jewish people of the way that God cared for them in the desert. The meal begins with the retelling of the Exodus story and then the youngest person present asks four questions which the oldest person answers. Before the Jewish people left Egypt, there wasn't time to wait for their bread to rise, so unleavened bread is served at the Seder along with salt water, a symbol of the slaves' tears. Wine is drunk four times during the meal as a reminder that God promised four times to bring the Jewish people out of Egypt and to freedom.

Passover Model

Much Israeli art celebrates Jewish traditions. The painting by Israeli artist Dora Holzhandler on page 56 is *The Passover Meal*. Discuss what happens during a Passover meal and use the painting as inspiration for making a 3-D model of a family celebrating a Passover meal.

Approach

1. Make up a salt dough mixture using two cups of flour to every cup of salt used. Slowly add water to make a pliable dough – not too dry and not too sticky.

2. Model items to go on the table for the Passover meal, for example, plates, serving platters, candlesticks, dishes and so on.

3. Place the dough items on a non-stick baking tray and bake in the oven at 150°C for 1–2 hours. Leave the dough models to cool in the oven.

4. Glue white kitchen roll on the box as a tablecloth.

5. Make pipe-cleaner figures and then wind wool around the body, arms and legs to represent clothing.

6. Cut oval shapes from felt, and glue onto the pipe-cleaner heads as faces. Use thin felt-tipped pen to add features to the faces. Add wool to the heads in different hairstyles.

7. Paint all the dough items and, when dry, glue them onto the tablecloth.

8. Make a carpet by gluing felt squares onto brown hessian board and create a background scene using part of a cardboard box painted to show the windows and furniture. Add detail with 3-D paints.

Resources
- Board covered with brown hessian
- Coloured felt
- Wallpaper samples
- Large cardboard box and smaller box for table
- White kitchen roll
- Plain flour, salt and water
- Mixing bowl and spoon
- Non-stick baking tray
- 3-D paints and paintbrushes
- Pipe-cleaners
- Coloured wool
- PVA glue
- Felt-tipped pens

Hanukkah

Jewish people celebrate Hanukkah to remember a time more than 2000 years ago when Jews in Ancient Israel weren't allowed to practise their faith. Judah, the Maccabee, led a revolt against the foreign rulers and he rededicated the Holy Temple. The word 'Hanukkah' means 'dedication'. The eternal lamp was re-lit and burned for eight days, although there was only enough oil for one day and so this was considered a miracle.

Only an eight-branched menorah (Hebrew for 'candlestick') can be used to celebrate the festival of Hanukkah. The candle on the furthest right-hand side is lit first and by the end of the week all eight candles are lit to commemorate the miracle of the oil in the Holy Temple. Each night, families gather to light the candles, sing songs and recite blessings. At Hanukkah, people eat foods cooked in oil such as doughnuts and latkes, which are potato cakes. Children may also be given chocolate coins with Jewish symbols on them.

Read *Light the Festive Candles* by Aileen Fisher on page 59 to inspire the children to write their own Hanukkah poems. Make a display showing a large papier mâché menorah.

Resources
- Cardboard
- Papier mâché pulp
- Silver and gold paint and paintbrushes
- Blue and yellow paper
- Gold foil
- Ballpoint pens

Approach

1. Draw an eight-branched menorah with eight candles on cardboard and cover with a layer of papier mâché pulp.

2. Allow the pulp to dry and harden and then paint with the silver and gold paint.

3. Draw circular coins on gold foil to represent the chocolate coins that are given to children at this festival. Draw Jewish symbols on the foil coins using a ballpoint pen to give an embossed effect.

4. Add yellow and blue paper circles at the top of each candle to represent the flame.

Light the Festive Candles

Light the first of eight tonight –
The farthest candle to the right.

Light the first and second, too,
When tomorrow's day is through.

Then light three, and then light four
Every dusk one candle more.

Till all eight burn bright and high,
Honouring a day gone by

When the Temple was restored,
Rescued from the Syrian lord,

And an eight-day feast proclaimed –
The Festival of Lights – well named

To celebrate the joyous day
When we regained the right to pray
To our one God in our own way.

Aileen Fisher

Beliefs

In the seventh century, the prophet Muhammad  founded the religion of Islam in Arabia. The followers of Islam are called Muslims and they believe in one God, Allah. Islamic life is based on the five pillars of Islam, a set of rules, which Muslims strictly follow so that they will gain a place in heaven. The first pillar is Shahadah, which is a statement of faith that says 'There is no God but Allah, and Muhammad is his prophet.' The second pillar is Salah, or prayer. The third pillar is Zakah, which is giving alms to the poor and needy. The fourth pillar requires Muslims to fast in the holy month of Ramadan and is called Sawm. The fifth pillar, Hajj, is the name given to the pilgrimage to Makkah. Makkah is the birthplace of Muhammad, and all Muslims try to visit Makkah at least once in their lifetime. The Ka'bah, a huge ancient black stone, is the sacred shrine that Muslims touch during their pilgrimage. The Ka'bah is covered with a black cloth, embroidered with verses from the Qur'an.

The Qur'an is the holy book of Islam and is used by Muslims as the guide for the way they live their lives. Studying the Qur'an, as well as being able to recite parts, is very important to Muslims. They believe that those who follow Allah faithfully will go to a heavenly paradise when they die. This wonderful place is a magnificent garden full of sweet-smelling flowers, singing birds and golden rocks covered with jewels.

Heavenly Paradise

Make a collage showing paradise as the children imagine it to look. In the foreground, show a Muslim praying.

Approach

1. Draw different exotic birds and decorate with coloured metallic foil, collage paper and feathers.

2. Fold the gold metallic foil paper to make gold stones and then glue on beads and stick-on jewels.

3. Draw and paint a Muslim praying on the cardboard box, adding gold patterned windows to the background.

4. Display the Muslim praying in front of the collage of Paradise.

Resources
- Large, rectangular cardboard box
- Paints and paintbrushes
- Coloured foil paper including gold
- Feathers
- Beads
- PVA glue
- Collage paper
- White paper
- Stick-on jewels

 This symbol is used after the name Muhammad as a sign of respect.

Whirling Dervishes

Sufism has been described as the name given to the spiritual heart of Islam. Dervishes, a class of Sufi Muslims, perform a special whirling dance as an expression of their faith. They use dance and chanting to reach out to Allah and become closer to him. 'Dervish' means 'poor', because the first Sufis were holy men who lived without any possessions.

Make a collage of whirling dervishes using dolly clothes pegs to represent the dancers and musicians.

Approach

1. Use black card for the background and add orange sponge printing to the area where the musicians sit.

2. Add lines using a gold metallic pen and then dust the background using white chalk.

3. Give each dolly clothes peg a face and hair using black felt-tipped pens.

4. Cut outfits from white felt for the dancers and red or brown felt for the musicians and glue onto the dolly pegs.

5. Make plasticine hats for all the dolly peg dancers and musicians and then stick into place on the black background using PVA glue.

6. Draw and cut instruments from sandpaper or make instruments from plasticine and stick in place on each musician.

7. Add a yellow corrugated card border to three sides as shown.

Resources
- Black card
- Gold metallic pens
- Orange paint and small sponges
- White chalk
- Dolly clothes pegs
- Black felt-tipped pins
- Terracotta plasticine
- White, red and brown felt
- Sandpaper
- PVA glue
- Yellow corrugated card

Places of Worship

The Muslim place of worship is the mosque. Before entering a mosque, Muslims must remove their shoes and wash their faces, hands and feet. Some mosques are very simple structures, others are grand and very ornate. Islam forbids realistic images of humans or other living things, and so the tiled walls of some mosques are decorated with intricate patterns and geometric shapes. Muslims pray facing the mihrab, an empty recess that shows the direction of Makkah. They kneel to pray with their heads touching the floor. Beside the mihrab is a pulpit called the minbar from which the imam gives the sermon and leads the prayers.

The imam is the leader of the Muslim congregation. He would be learned in both the Qur'an and the Hadith. The prayers would be said in Arabic and accompanied by movements called rak'ahs. The imam performs the rak'ahs, copied by the congregation.

Mosque Model

Resources
- Large cardboard box
- 3-D paints
- Paints and paintbrushes
- Large, flat piece of cardboard
- Gold stick-on stars
- Modroc
- Card
- Water tray
- Silver spray-paint

Approach

1. Paint the cardboard box brown and, when dry, decorate it with 3-D paints, showing arched doors and intricate windows.

2. Make a domed roof from cardboard and cover it with modroc strips soaked in water for 2–3 seconds. Allow to dry and harden and then spray silver.

3. Paint a background onto the large, flat piece of cardboard showing two minarets and a starry sky.

4. Assemble the mosque and display as shown.

Islamic Tiles

The Qur'an forbids images of any kind to be made of Allah, Muhammad 🕌 or other prophets as it is felt that no image could be good enough to reflect the magnificence of Allah's creation. For this reason, Islamic artists have concentrated on developing beautiful geometric patterns. Ceramic tiles are a favourite kind of decoration on Islamic buildings. Many tiles bear patterns that are based on plant forms. The flowers, leaves and stems are made into more abstract designs in typical Islamic style. Calligraphy is used to create pictures in the shapes of animals and there is a well-used image, a boat, which is known as the Ship of Life.

Resources
- White paper
- Glass mirror tiles
- Glass paints or glass markers

Approach

1. Look at pictures of patterned tiles in the Islamic style and then ask the children to design a square tile on paper.

2. Copy the design onto a glass tile using glass paints or glass markers, which are as simple to work with as felt-tipped pens, and give a wonderful effect on glass.

63

Stories and Paintings

At the festival of Laylat-ul-Qadr, Muslims prepare themselves for the feast of Ramadan. The story of King Hakim on page 65 is told around the time of this festival.

Garden collage

Make two collages on felt backgrounds, one of King Hakim's garden and one of the widow's garden.

Resources

- Different-coloured felts, including two large green pieces for the backgrounds
- Plain flour, salt and water
- Mixing bowl and spoon
- Paints and paintbrushes
- PVA glue
- White paper
- Non-stick baking tray
- Clay tools

Approach

1. Cut lots of different vegetable shapes from the felt for the widow's garden, and flower and tree shapes for the king's garden.

2. Glue these vegetable and flower shapes onto the appropriate backgrounds.

3. Make up a salt dough mixture using two cups of flour to every cup of salt used. Slowly add water to make a pliable dough – not too dry and not too sticky.

4. Roll out the dough and use clay tools or pastry cutters to cut out tree, flower and vegetable shapes.

5. Place the dough items on a non-stick baking tray and bake in a low oven (150°C) for 1–2 hours. Leave in the oven to cool.

6. Paint the dough flowers and trees. When dry, glue them onto the collage.

7. Make the characters from paper and decorate with fabric. Attach these to the garden collages.

King Hakim's Garden

King Hakim had a beautiful garden full of different flowers, trees and shrubs. The widow next door to him did not grow flowers, instead she grew all kinds of vegetables, which the king did not regard as pleasant to sit and look out on. The king decided that he would like to buy the widow's garden and build a summerhouse or a pond, but the widow refused to sell, saying that the vegetables were her livelihood. The chief advisor to the king offered her bags of gold and then a chest full of gold, but the widow said that she would not part with her garden for all the gold in the kingdom. The king became so angry that he told his soldiers to take the garden by force. The widow shouted to Allah for help and then she ran to find the qadi, the local judge. When the qadi returned with the widow, her vegetables were being dug up and taken away. The king asked the qadi what he should do with his new garden and the qadi said that all work should cease at once and they should meet the next day to discuss the matter.

The next day the qadi arrived in the king's part of the garden with a donkey and some sacks. The qadi apologised for bringing his donkey into the garden, but asked the king a favour. The qadi asked to fill his sacks full of soil from the king's garden for his own garden. The king agreed and ordered his gardeners to help. The soldiers helped the gardeners by loading the sacks onto the donkey until the donkey almost collapsed under the weight of the soil. The king asked the qadi why he wanted more soil than he could carry away, and the qadi replied that he was only doing what the king himself had done to the unhappy widow. He explained to the king that the soil represents their sins, and when they die they will all face Allah on the Day of Judgement carrying all their sins. He said that Allah would see their sins and those with sins would be unable to enter paradise. The king realised what the qadi was trying to tell him and he asked for Allah's forgiveness. The king also asked the widow for her forgiveness and told the gardeners to re-plant all her vegetables, tidy up her garden and give her a chest of gold. The qadi managed to resolve the situation and keep everybody happy.

Ms C-23 fol.43b *An old man and a young man in front of the tents of the rich pilgrims, from 'The Maqamat'* (*The Meetings*) by Al-Hariri (1054–1121) c.1240 (vellum), Persian School, (13th century)/Institute of Oriental Studies, St Petersburg, Russia/ www.bridgeman.co.uk

The Road to Makkah

This thirteenth-century picture shows a group of rich pilgrims. It is the duty of every Muslim to go on Hajj to Makkah at least once in their lifetime. The pilgrims in the picture are wearing colourful clothes and rest in colourful tents, but will soon put on the simple white clothes called ihram. Pilgrims must be in a special state of holiness, achieved by washing and declaring their faith. Men wear two large pieces of seamless, unstitched white cloth as a sign that they are all equal. Their pilgrimage involves visiting the Ka'bah, the stone monument thought to have been built by Ibrahim and his son Isma'il.

Road to Makkah Display

Talk about why Muslims try to make a pilgrimage to Makkah. Make a display showing the pilgrims on the road to Makkah, inspired by the picture on page 66.

Approach

1. Draw around a camel template on brown sugar paper and add camels to the sugar paper backgrounds. On the background, staple a wavy pattern to create a 3-D effect.

2. Glue the tents to the background and add stick-on stars to the night sky.

Resources
- Wallpaper samples
- Coloured sugar paper
- Collage materials
- Stick-on stars
- PVA glue
- Camel template

Festivals and Ceremonies

A Muslim Marriage

Many Muslim marriages are still arranged by the families of the couple. If the marriage is to go ahead, a Muslim man often gives his bride-to-be a dowry, which can be a payment in money or property. This is sometimes given to the bride-to-be in a beautiful dowry box.

Marriage is seen as a binding agreement before God and the ceremony can be held anywhere, often at the bride's home. The preparations for the wedding take a long time. The day before the wedding, the bride's hands and feet may be adorned with elaborate, traditional henna designs. These patterns are said to symbolise strength and love. The bride will often dress in red for the ceremony with lots of gold jewellery. The ceremony begins with a reading from the fourth chapter of the Qur'an, al Nisá, and next follows a talk on the duties of marriage. The couple then agree to the marriage three times and rings are exchanged, followed by a blessing. The man then takes his bride and guests to enjoy a wedding feast.

Approach

1. Draw and paint the Muslim couple, before adding fabrics to enhance the work.

2. Add garlands of pressed flowers around their necks.

3. Ask the children to draw around their hands on card, and then to cut these shapes out. Decorate the hands and feet with henna designs using 3-D paints.

4. Display the couple, surrounded by the hands and feet as shown.

Resources
- Card
- Fabrics
- PVA glue
- 3-D paints
- Paints and paintbrushes
- Pressed flowers
- Gold stick-on stars

Dowry Purses

Resources
- Felt squares
- Fabric crayons
- Pins, needles and sewing thread
- Sequinned material
- Stick-on jewels
- PVA glue

Approach

1. Decorate a felt square with Islamic-inspired designs using fabric crayons.

2. Fold three sides to form an envelope shape, pin in place and then oversew.

3. Decorate with stick-on jewels; add sequinned material to the inside as required.

Dowry Boxes

Resources
- Small cardboard boxes
- Paints and paintbrushes
- 3-D paints

Approach

1. Paint the boxes and allow to dry.

2. Decorate with Islamic designs using 3-D paints.

Islamic Festivals

The two main Islamic festivals are Id-ul-Fitr and Id-ul-Adha. Ramadan is the ninth month of the Islamic calendar. During Ramadan, Muslims fast between sunrise and sunset. Id-ul-Fitr is the festival which takes place at the end of Ramadan. Presents and cards are exchanged and there are celebratory meals with friends and relatives. Muslims attend special prayers at the mosque and give thanks for Allah's blessings. Berlie Doherty's poem *Idh Mubarak!*, which means 'Happy Id!', (on page 71) will help the children to understand how the festival is celebrated. Use the poem to inspire a collage of the child Safuran in traditional Islamic clothes dancing in her garden. Border the collage with Id Mubarak cards, remembering that Arabic is written from right to left, and so Id cards are folded on the right-hand side.

Id Mubarak Cards

Resources
- Silver foil
- Pearlescent paints and paintbrushes
- A4 coloured card
- PVA glue

Approach

1. Decorate the cards with drawings of a mosque, a garden, the moon and stars, or just an intricate pattern. The cards are usually colourful – blue and gold being the most popular colours as they symbolise heaven and the sun.

2. Paint the designs with pearlescent paints and add silver foil as required.

Safuran Collage

Resources
- Paints and small sponges
- Silver paper
- White paper
- Textured fabrics including red
- Stick-on stars
- PVA glue

Approach

1. Draw and sponge-paint a picture of Safuran dancing in the garden with a mosque in the background. Paint a new moon in the sky and add stick-on stars.

2. Add red fabric to Safuran's shalwar-zameeze and fabric of another colour for her dupatta scarf.

3. Add the Id Mubarak cards around the edge of the painting as shown.

Idh Mubarak!

Maghrib is the name of the dusk
After the sun goes down
And Safuran is the child in the garden
Watching for the new moon.

It's here! The moon's come! It's Idh!
Idh Mubarak! She calls.

Her shalwar-zameeze is like poppies
Her dupatta scarf drifts like a breeze
Her bangles gleam as she dances
Idh Mubarak! She says.

Her family take gifts to the mosque
Today let no one be sad
Let no one be left out of the feasting
Idh Mubarak! Instead.

At home there are cards and presents
And smells of spices and sweets
And the women rush to get ready
The great Idh feast.

Dad reminds them that under the stars
Of Africa, Pakistan, India,
Bangladesh
This is the day of happiness
And under
The stars of England, Safuran says,
Watching her moon. Praise
Be to Allah, Dad says. Praise him.
And eat!

Bismillahir Rahmanir Rahim.
Idh Mubarak
Happy Idh!

Berlie Doherty

Sekaten Maulud

In Indonesia, the celebration of the Prophet Muhammad's birthday is known as Sekaten Maulud. There is a procession in which traditional foods are carried through the streets to the mosque. In one town, Yogyakarta, a team of men carry a huge dish of rice and cakes to the mosque for everybody to share. People visit the tombs of important religious leaders, and prayers are said at the mosque.

Make a wax and ink batik showing this festival.

Approach

Resources
- White sugar paper
- Wax crayons
- Drawing inks and paintbrushes
- An iron

1. Draw a picture showing a team of men carrying food to the mosque.

2. Colour the picture using wax crayons.

3. Carefully screw up the picture to crack the wax and then flatten it out by hand.

4. Paint over the whole picture using drawing inks and allow to dry.

5. Iron the painting between sheets of white sugar paper.

⚠️ **Note:** An adult should use the iron at all times.